Dear Gretchen

LETTERS TO MY DOG

Heidi Parker Colonna

THAYER STREET
PUBLISHING

THAYER STREET PUBLISHING

Copyright © 2021 by Heidi Parker Colonna
Photographs © 2021 by Heidi Parker Colonna

Publisher's Cataloging-In-Publication Data
(Prepared by The Donohue Group, Inc.)

Names: Colonna, Heidi Parker, author.
Title: Dear Gretchen : letters to my dog / by Heidi Parker Colonna.
Description: [Westfield, Massachusetts] : Thayer Street Publishing, [2021]
Identifiers: ISBN 9798985146905 (paperback) | ISBN 9798985146912 (ebook)
Subjects: LCSH: Colonna, Heidi Parker. | Dog owners-- Biography. | Human-animal relationships. | Grief. | LCGFT: Autobiographies.
Classification: LCC SF422.82.C65 A3 2021 (print) | LCC SF422.82.C65 (ebook) | DDC 636.70092--dc23

Cover design by Sam Alam

To contact the publisher for any reason, including for information on bulk purchases, please email thayerstreetpublishing@gmail.com.

Dedication

THIS BOOK IS DEDICATED TO MY MOTHER,
PATRICIA, WHO SHOWED ME
THE MAGIC IN EVERYDAY OCCURRENCES.

Contents

Acknowledgments

I would like to express gratitude to my first reader: my mother, Patricia Harmon. She brought Gretchen into my life and made her miracle known to me 20 years later. When I finally got the story down, she responded with her usual excitement that made me keep going in the long and tedious editing process. An author herself, she was there for that, too, and helped me choose the title. The cover photo choice is hers.

Thank you to the readers who followed and helped improve the manuscript: my niece, voracious reader and dog lover Gianna DiClementi Crean; friend and former HSUS writing colleague Cathy Vincenti; friend, mentor, and former English professor Marion W. Copeland; Pam Peebles, former colleague from the shelter from which Gretchen hailed, who still works tirelessly for animals and families; and Nicole Forsyth, my boss at RedRover, a nonprofit that brings animals out of crisis and strengthens the human-animal bond. Thank you to Dr. Andrew Hersman of East Springfield Veterinary Hospital, whose father Richard was Gretchen's vet, for providing the medical perspective; I consider them both family. Family friend Susan Greaney not only read, but as one who provided a second home for Gretchen, shared invaluable memories, and reconnected me with Gretchen's puppyhood rescuer, Claudia Hurley. My stepfather, Bill Harmon, named and loved Gretchen and provided his own memory and support for this project. My father, John W.K. Parker, friend to Gretchen and all dogs, was the first to cry over my stories.

I'm grateful for the friendship, encouragement, and critiques of the members of my Manuscript Academy Creative Nonfiction Writers' Group: Lisa Fabish, Diane Herbert, Maggie Marton, and Chrissy Holm. Thanks to the support of the WhipCity Wordsmiths, especially founder Susan Buffum and author Shawn P. Flynn whose heartfelt book, *The Kitty Who Rescued Me After I Rescued Him*, beckoned me to bring my own beloved pet's story to the front burner.

A special thanks to my husband Al and sons Kevin and AJ for cheering me on to chase my longtime dream of publishing something of my own. They popped into writers' meetings, tolerated my "lost in story" stares, and took care of things when I had to hole up and get the words down.

And of course Gretchen, my sister- and forever-dog: Thank you for saving me with your gentle presence—not once but twice—and for living the best stories ever with me. More than anything, thank you for never saying goodbye, because I love you too much for that.

INTRODUCTION

Softer Than Velvet

March 18, 1985

My feet were masters of the stairs with the painted-on pawprints. I no longer had to look to follow them down, past the front desk, to the dog room. A lady was backing out with a mop bucket, and the *Personnel Only* door closed. Whatever that meant. I was nine. But I knew this:

It was MINE! The dog room was MINE!!!

I scanned the eyes in the cages that circled me, breathed in the smell of bleach and my favorite animal, and felt a smile come. My bubble-gum-pink hi-top Reeboks slid on the wet cement in a twirl, and I hung my head back to take in the barks bouncing off the cement walls.

There was lanky *RODNEY*, a machine-gun barker in one of the big floor cages at the far end of the kennel, a

1 YR. OLD MALE HOUND MIX, the card said. When I came close, he lifted his head.

"Arooooooooooooooo!"

"Aroooooooo!" I exclaimed back into his red-brown eyes. "Hi Rodney! You're almost as tall as *me*!"

Next was *Bella*, a *3 MOS. OLD FEMALE LAB MIX* with paws up on her door. I plunked down on my butt and wrapped my fingers around the two chain link diamonds where her little black toe pads poked out.

"Black beauty." My whisper turned into a giggle as she stuck her nose through a diamond in the middle.

I wanted Bella.

I wanted Rodney.

I looked down the row of eyes that kept going.

I WANTED ALL OF THEM.

I would *take* all of them, but no way would Mom say yes to that. I tried to think through the barking and pawing and jangling of cage doors. That's when I noticed a bowl but no eyes in one of the shining metal cat-sized cages stacked up in the corner back toward the lobby door. I was finally tall enough to stand with my sneakers flat on the ground and see inside. Beyond the bowl, sleepy breaths rippled across a puppy belly. A tiny black triangle ear flopped over an eye; the other smushed beneath her on the pink towel she lay on.

What sticks with me most about that day, even more than the adorableness, is the peace within the depths of that tiny cage that was like a world of its own in the chaos of that kennel, and the feeling in my center that erased all the chaos in my brain about who I should take home that day.

I heard the door to the lobby squeak open and slam behind me before a loud string of voices:

"OH!"

"AWWWW!"

I turned long enough to make out two girls about my biggest sister's age. And I guess they thought I found something good, because they were coming. I froze, felt a punch to my chest move to my throat, and remembered what the Saturday afternoon volunteers said on visits with my dad and older brother Rocky: *You need the cage card to do an adoption application.* A dog would go nowhere without it. But my brain had nothing to do with what happened next.

I pulled the card that said *CLOVER 8 WKS-OLD FEMALE SHEPHERD MIX* up from the shining metal holder and darted through the squeaky door.

"WE WANT THIS ONE!!!!!!"

I couldn't believe the words came out to a strange adult, loud enough to make her look back at me. I couldn't believe I was there, my body smushed against the counter that separated staff from public, holding a lined index card high, the distress flag of a kid without a dog.

"Okay, Hun!" I read *DONNA*'s nametag as she said it.

I looked over to Mom, in from the parking lot after dropping me at the door. She had already laid out on the counter her last house tax bill and driver's license that we'd need for an adoption, the blonde-frosted goddess that she was.

"I was just telling your mom about the deworming and vaccinations that we do for dogs."

None of which mattered, if we didn't get *this* dog.

Donna looked at the card I'd just smacked down.

"But we can take…CLOVER out now and let you spend some time with her."

I led the way to find the older girls laughing and holding Rodney's paws through his door. Clover was standing, her black-lined eyes squinting at me as she dropped down at her cage door, a string tail swooshing on the blanket behind her. Donna pulled up the latch, letting the door swing out, and went to hang one of those lasso leashes over her head, but I had already scooped her in my arms like a baby. I felt her weight—She was so light!—and fuzziness in my hands. My back straightened. I looked at her tiny face and held the top of her head with my free hand. Her ears were softer than the velvet inside my jewelry box.

"I got her," I said to Donna, who smiled, like we must have looked cute together.

"I guess you do!"

A Time to Take

"Bill is OK with this?" I asked Mom as we headed west toward the Berkshire Mountains that made a dark line against the sky, Clover warming my lap. My new stepfather was not exactly a puppy kind of person.

"This was my decision Heidi," she replied.

My eyes widened before the mahogany dashboard of Mom's new Lincoln Continental. She looked at me through her huge brown sunglasses that matched the car.

"Just don't you worry about it Chickie," she said using my baby nickname. "Each person has to give and take in a marriage. It was a huge sacrifice for all of us to move for Bill. Now it's our turn to *take*."

I thought about it. She had noticed how sad I was when I said my belly hurt that morning, and when I asked for a dog again. Rocky and I had been working this huge dog begging campaign since we realized we weren't getting our old life back, and now Mom was finally done saying no. *That's* why she finally took me to the shelter in Springfield.

"But Bill didn't want *Oliver*," I said, my voice breaking as I thought of my dog—my *old* dog—from our *old* town.

Mom gunned it up our new hill, which was more like a mountain. Our new blue house appeared, with its porch along the side, jutting straight back like an arrow to the front door that met the garage and made a dark little corner. Clover yawned and looked up at me, her eyes the color of maple syrup with sun shining through the bottle.

"I told you Oliver was nuts," Mom said. "His new family has *time* for a dog like that."

I pictured Oliver jumping at the hood of her old Subaru in our old driveway, mouthing at the white clutch purse she put there as she kissed me goodbye for a real estate appointment. He took it straight into a mud puddle. He might have been nuts. And Mom might have had a lot going on with four wild kids, and now we were getting two stepsisters. But Oliver was mine. He was tiny like Clover once.

"Oliver had to go—Bill or no Bill, move or no move. Just don't you worry about it Chickie."

"Did you see?" Mom yelled to Bill from the stove that night after he clinked his keys at the door and they did their gross kiss on the lips. Clover was sleeping again in the corner of the kitchen, in a banana box leftover from the move.

"Heidi and I went to the animal shelter today."

I listened from the family room next door, which he had quickly moved into before switching the TV from Fraggle Rock to the stock channel.

"Did you," he said, talking back to the kitchen door. Bill had a deep ogre voice that always came out with a layer of sweet frosting on it for Mom.

"Yes, and we found this calm little dog," she said.

"Is that right, Patty."

"Do you want to see her?"

He disappeared back to the kitchen and I was on my feet, watching him peer into the banana box, his Barron's newspaper folded up in his hand.

"Aren't you a cute little thing," he said, the frosting still on his voice.

"Isn't she? We want you to name her," Mom said with a wink to me, just like we talked about earlier. We thought he'd take it better that way.

He stood there and thought for a bit.

"She looks like a German Shepherd," he said. "Why don't we give her a nice German name."

And then my new stepfather put a permanent name to the angel who became mine a week before my tenth birthday.

"Gretchen."

The first pictures I took of Gretchen (clockwise from top left): in my brothers' arms at my 10th birthday party, March 1985; on our kitchen floor; lounging in the side yard of our new house

Lucky Clover

As Gretchen grew, her German Shepherd look faded, but her peace did not. When the sad wail of the horn of the train, coming from my old home, made its way up the hill and through the backyard woods, she let me lay my head on her side, and rocked it with swells of black-streaked-brown fur. She'd sit by my side on the steps of the front porch of our new blue house as I sized up the maze of pavement and people on our new hill—like the older boy who called my new puppy "Clover."

"No," I said. "It's Gretchen...Why did you say Clover?"

"We found her," he said. "Outside my swim meet in Rhode Island, before St. Patrick's Day. That's why we named her 'Clover.' My mom brought her back with us to Massachusetts."

I didn't think to ask the neighbor boy's name, or his mother's—this woman who brought my puppy to me. I learned later that it was Claudia, and she was my new friend Jessica's godmother.

But on that day in 1985, I just stood, wrapped my puppy's leash tightly around my hand, and said, "Oh. Well, she's Gretchen now. She's my dog."

Document	Date	Breed	Color
Adoption form	3/18/85	Shep/lab	Brown/blk
Rabies Vaccination Certificate	7/17/85	ShepX	TAN/BLK
Certificate of Neutering a Female Dog	7/18/85	Labrador and Shepherd	Gold
Rabies Vaccination Certificate	7/11/86	Mix/Collie	Brown
Dog License	4/3/87	Collie	Brown
Dog License	4/28/88	mixed	Brown

Gretchen's health and licensing documents and these photos show her German Shepherd look fading fast. We never found out what her breed truly was.

Free Bird

It's a good thing Gretchen was my dog, because I needed her. Our whole newly-mixed-up family did. We needed her cup of peace thrown into the blender of big personalities and opinions that churned in our new blue house. Gretchen would not even let out a whine or whimper or bark to be let out or in. She'd gently knock her front paw on the back sliding door to announce her arrival after using the restroom she'd made out of the wooded part of our backyard (because she'd never mess up the grass). She'd smile and wag no matter who walked in the front door. Her peace was free for the taking, there on the carpet by the slider where she lay, no matter the dinnertime squabble or tension in the air above her.

And it was a good thing Gretchen was ours, because we gave her the two main ingredients for any animal's welfare past food, water, and shelter: love and freedom. She could have used her freedom to lay on the porch or dart straight into the side of a pickup truck like another dog might, but she used it very wisely. She hooked up with a Brittany Spaniel mix from the next street named Hugo. Hugo knew the whole neighborhood from his regular rounds with the morning lady walkers' group. When he laid eyes on Gretchen, he let his ladies keep walking. Together, Gretchen and Hugo went farther than they'd ever go on their own, through the maze of little side streets, into the woods, to two different rivers at the bottom of our hill below the Berkshires in Western Massachusetts. Hugo and I hit it off right away, and I happily became one of them—until they became like two flying birds taken off through a backyard or deep into the woods, and my 10-year-old toothpick legs surrendered. So I'd wait for them to return, their undersides covered in river mud.

My childhood view of friendship with Gretchen and Hugo, in our backyard after a river run

Mom captured Gretchen and me at our backyard picnic table

If Gretchen was out too late and we didn't answer her knock on the sliding door, she'd run to my friend Jessica's and bark below the master bedroom window. Mrs. Greaney would descend, wipe her paws, and roll out her version of a red carpet: a sheet on the comforter. Once Bill went to retrieve our dog the next morning and smelled scrambled eggs on the stove. He thought he might get an invite to the table, but that was for Gretchen.

Adventurous dogs are bound to meet with danger, and it came one day on our hill. Rocky and I found Gretchen standing at the sliding door, Hugo by her side and blood streaming down a back leg. We scooped her up in an old blanket and woke our biggest sister for a frantic ride back to Springfield, to the hospital above the shelter. After a surgical repair from a hit-by-car, we got her home, one leg propped up in a gigantic bright white cast. Hugo was already there waiting at the back deck, and patiently walked beside her up the steps. I patted her bed by the sliding door, got my markers out and drew a half rainbow with a cloud and my name on her cast. I lay there with her and helped her out to pee, until she could fly like a bird again.

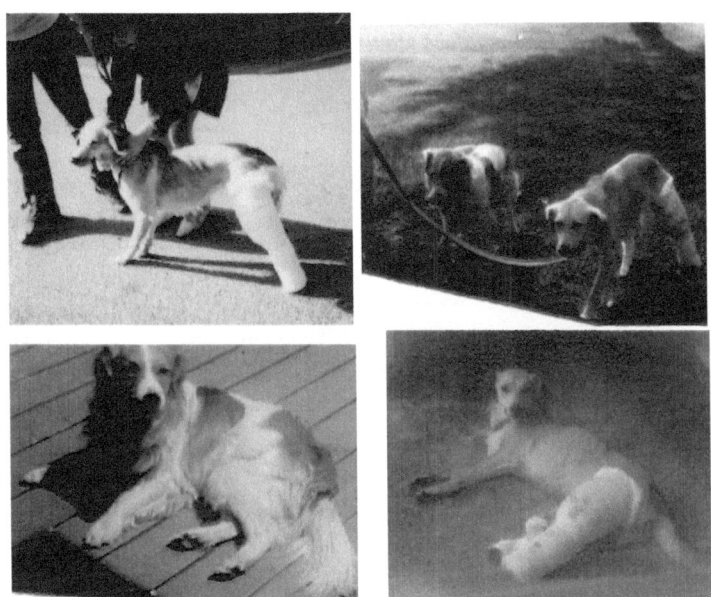

Clockwise from top left: Fixing Gretchen's collar in the hospital parking lot; Hugo walking her to the deck stairs; back home with her cast signed; Hugo waiting on the other side of the sliding door   c· 1986

Leaving the Hill

In high school, I got a boyfriend of my own named Conor and a fast car to speed off on my own adventures. After selling the lots of our expanding subdivision on the hill, Mom got a powerboat and fulfilled her dream of cruising the New England shoreline any chance she could. My siblings grew up and left, and Mom, Bill, Gretchen, and I moved again—to Southwick, a town on the Connecticut line with an even denser forest. Hugo-time dwindled to seldom visits. I went to college locally and volunteered at the shelter that brought us Gretchen.

Gretchen became a senior, her fur lightening from brown to red, then gold. Her body became boxier, then thinner. I lolled in the backyard sun with her and a Giants football she stole from the new neighbor's garage and captured her in photographs, knowing the end was not far away, thinking with every snap, *I can't do it. I cannot say goodbye to her.* I busied myself, completing my last year of an animal science degree and starting a job at Springfield's other 24-hour emergency animal hospital. Working daily amidst suffering and death, I tried to prepare myself for the impossible: of watching my own beloved go through what the animals in front of me were.

Conor and I bought a three-family home in a city next to Springfield. We got married, and I bounced back and forth between my new life and my old dog who I'd left in the comfort of Mom and Bill's sprawling ranch house in the country. I listened to the vets talking about the latest medications for arthritis and dementia and oversaw Gretchen's vet appointments and prescriptions. I came back to stay for a while when I knew her last breath was near. It was July 2, 1999. Her ears were still as soft.

Gretchen and me in Southwick, 1998

The First Letter

My first letter to Gretchen was penned as she faded from this world, with the nearest materials I could find: a half-used one-subject notebook and Bic pen from Mom's desk. I needed to protest the inevitable. I needed to feel out a new avenue of communication with my best friend. For 14 years, Gretchen and I didn't need the written word. We didn't need the spoken word. All we needed was presence—side by side on the ground in a sun patch on one of Mom's thick oriental rugs was best—but now she had to go. Her body had given out, so much that I couldn't watch her suffer another day. I called the vet to request a house-call euthanasia, and she could come "now," she said, on the Friday of July Fourth weekend.

Adrenaline fueled the pen. I was exhausted from my attempts to counter Gretchen's legs giving out and other breakdowns of her body, and now she would soon be off to Heaven, a far-away place that I wouldn't reach til *my* body gave out. At 24 years old, that would be forever. My tears dropped like fat rain on bleeding blue ink. This was the disaster of my young life. I had to say goodbye and lay out what she meant to me and what her absence would mean for my future as she lay down the hall, all in the time it took for the vet to drive from the next town over.

Like the Jim Croce ballad "I'll Have to Say I Love You in a Song" that I'd sing for her in my new loneliness, a letter was what I had. It was going to be "kinda late" to communicate like we used to. Songs and letters and prayers would be what I was left with. So I pulled a Kleenex from my pocket, sopped up the tears, and finished my letter. I carefully pulled out the lined paper and folded it up in a triangle, like one of those paper footballs you exchange in class—not to throw to my best friend's desk, but to wrap in tape to protect it from moisture and bugs and to throw in her grave, dug by Bill and my sister Cookie behind the wood pile where Mom had taken our smiling picture just months before.

With every breathtaking sob and second-guessed effort to end her pain, I dropped all my love with Gretchen in a perfectly-wrapped triangle, and sent her off before setting off on my emptiness.

What I didn't know is that over the next five years of doubt and suffering and not writing letters, her love would not falter. Of course it wouldn't. I didn't know that one day, she'd find a way to show her girl her love, too.

She is my soul mate—we connected like no two other people. We had similar personalities and were the very best of friends! To think of her makes me cry, no matter how normal I know her death was.
I miss being with her—such a unique being—nobody else like her.
But dogs don't live long enough.

Diary entry, December 29, 1999

1

Five Years Later

July 2, 2004

The sandy cliffs appeared in the distance, familiar sentinels of our favorite vacation spot. Six days on Block Island, Rhode Island, were in front of me. Six days of no multitasking in my communications job for The Humane Society of the United States. Six days of no Hartford traffic and no 60-mile commute.

On this day, I was an idle passenger on a gliding ferry.

I got up from my seat next to my husband Conor, put all my weight on the railing of the front deck and let out a breath as loud as the sea winds.

Oh, these winds.

Five years ago I sat alone like cargo, red-eyed and unshowered on a lifejacket compartment back near the stairs, letting these winds have their way with my long, greasy dark hair. I looked into the whipping air that was the great nowhere above Block Island Sound and tried to picture her spirit swirling there. It felt more like a vacuum than a space occupied by my best friend.

No toughening of the heart I'd experienced at the animal hospital could spare me the grief of losing my sidekick. I hadn't grieved in the silence of my old bedroom the night after Gretchen died, in the sleepy woods of Southwick where I'd slept beside her the night before, like I should have—like I should have for the last years of her life, not just the last days. Instead, I had hopped in a car that was Block Island bound, with my sister-in-law and her friend. I aimed there like a homing pigeon, toward Mom and Conor. I'd made an escape from the pain. My best friend and little sister and daughter were gone. Gretchen was all those things to me.

On this day, the five-year anniversary of Gretchen's death, the winds whipped just as hard at the front of the ship. Mom's straw-blond hair waved like a flag at the ferry dock in Old Harbor, the same spot where she'd given me a hug and kissed my head and said, "Poor Chick" on July 2, 1999. She couldn't stand to be there for the sadness that took place in Gretchen's dog bed at the foot of her own bed.

As our sneakers clicked the joints of the metal gangway to the dock, I spotted Mom's larger-than-life smile, just like my late Papa's. The high cheekbones that pulled her mouth up so much. She was always more excited than most by the little things: a drive somewhere new, my first puppy Oliver anticipating his bowl of kibble as I walked it out to him, or eating on new tableware for the first time.

Isn't this fun? was her slogan.

"Chickie-Dee!" Mom said, "You look cute. Give me your head."

I tried to match one-tenth of her smile, and gave over the top of my head so she could grab it with both hands and kiss my forehead. It would be marked for the day with her wine-colored lipstick. We did our signature little dance whenever we greeted, bopping up and down from our knees with the kisses.

"You too Conor," she said, and started her excited sing-song slogan for us:

"Two cute little kids!"

We jumped in her minivan and started the 20-mile-an-hour parade to Payne's dock, to Mom's world. She loved boats since she could walk. Her first was a rowboat she found near Breckwood Lake in Springfield which wasted no time sinking to the bottom. As a teenager, she took one whiff of the sea by the yachts on a stroll down a Cape Cod dock with Papa, and that was it. After two upgrades from her first powerboat, she had her all-time favorite yacht: a 40-foot Diesel trawler with classic lines and gunwales for walking along the sides. My oldest sister Nellie helped pick a good drinking name—Last Call—because every dock I've been on kept the drinks flowing like the tides.

Mom loved celebration, and it was found in every corner of Block Island this time of year. The annual July 4th parade. Friends at Payne's. Mudslides at the Oar Restaurant looking over New Harbor. Of all the little islands and harbors she'd wandered into in clear skies or in fog, this was the one she kept coming back to. This was the one she brought all of us to, charting us out in shifts over two weeks centered around the fourth.

She swerved around a cluster of bikes taking up half the sandy road that was the main drag. I could feel the moisture-filled BI air drift in my open window and make my hair go frizzy. That's what made the blue hydrangeas crowding the storefronts so enormous their stalks barely kept the flowers afloat.

"What's this guy doing?" she said, coming to a halt as a man on a scooter came out past his stop sign at the four-way intersection, before inching onto Corn Neck Road.

"Nellie and the kids are showering from the beach," she said, alternating her eyes from the road to the stores and restaurants. "Remember Yellow Kittens?"

We glided past the familiar sign. It looks innocent, three kittens playing with yarn, but this is the island's heavy duty dance club at night, my big sisters' kind of heavy duty.

"The stories, yes," I said. "How could I forget."

The grasses along the road sway as if to wave you in to Block Island State Beach, with waves perfect for jumping and body surfing. This is where we were five years ago tonight: Nellie and her husband Gabe and Conor and me. I have the picture of me squinting my puffy eyes in a smile. I hadn't even packed a bag, and Nellie was generous: In the picture, I'm wearing her jean overall shorts and nautical blue and white striped shirt.

Nellie and I'd been the first crew for years now. My other sister Cookie and brother Rocky took a later shift. And then there was Mom's fifth kid: Nellie's best friend Winnie. We all called her Winnie, but Mom used her whole name in all caps and an exclamation point any time she addressed her, which only made sense given Winnie's huge personality: WINIFRED! Winnie was part of all our childhood shenanigans back when Mom was single. Sleepovers that ended with Winnie waking up with a gumball in her mouth. "Borrowing" the car when no one had a license. "Borrowing" from Mom's booze cabinet. Winnie was the funny one, the physical comic who could "do" Mom so well, putting on her mom voice barking orders and her real estate voice answering the phone. She *got* Mom, and she was the fifth kid Mom always wanted. Mom's decorative plate of a goddess holding two children in each arm and one climbing up her front that she proudly displayed on the fireplace mantel was proof of it.

"So what day is Winnie coming?" I asked.

"I don't think she's going to make it this year," Mom said, turning her head away to the salt pond off to her side of the van.

Winnie was under a dark spell as long as I was, only hers was darkening since her divorce. She'd fallen from our radar more and more, and now was the time we wanted to see her the most. She was expecting his first child.

"Look at this ass!" Mom screamed as a biker swerved toward the middle of the road. "Don't they know this is a road for cars, too!"

"Anyway," Mom said, snapping back into character. "Isn't this fun? I hope it doesn't rain for you kids! They're saying we might get something this afternoon."

After two quick turns, we squeezed into a spot behind a Land Rover-turned cow, complete with spots and a huge udder hanging from the rear bumper. Portable hibachi grills littered the sidewalk against the harbor.

"Hi Cow Car!" I said.

"See, we got the good spot this year," Mom said as she led the way toward the docks. "All I had to do was radio ahead to Cliff and he saved it for me."

There she was—the Last Call—on the second dock in, backed in perfect for Nan to step in and out of. Everyone else came and went in shifts, but Nan got the whole two weeks.

"Chickie-Poo-I-Love You!"

I heard her chipper voice singing as soon as our feet jostled the boat. We squeezed our duffel bags through the director's chairs on the deck to find her in her purple Hanes sweatshirt in her usual position, in the center of the loveseat holding a *Country Home* magazine open.

"Connie!"

Nana had nicknamed all of us.

"Nan!" We said in unison and sat beside her, our bags still attached, as Mom recited her inventory.

"Now I've got grape and strawberry coolers and beer," She announced from behind the breakfast bar in the step-down galley. "Or I can make you a drink. You're on Block Island!"

I took a seat on the couch next to Nan and held my strawberry bottle that had already began to sweat, but Nana would not take off that sweatshirt. She loved being *werm*, she said in her Irish accent.

"How's my Chick," she said, touching my leg. "You're so soft!"

I grabbed her hand, and the emotion flooded out.

"It's five years, Nan."

I heard the wind come out of her.

"Is it five years?"

I shook my head and felt stomach hollow out at the thought of Gretchen gone, dropped my head sideways into Nan's arms, and breathed out the pain into her own age-spotted softness. Nan had been there, with her quiet wisdom at the edge of Mom's bed like she was for every death in our family. Conor settled into the leather swivel club chair, careful not to spill his screwdriver. He wasn't there with me and Gretchen on July 2, 1999, but he was good to her. He got down on Gretchen's level and shared sticks with her, gnawing on the opposite end. He put treats up on Mom's butcher block and coaxed her paws up to get them. We'd called Conor her boyfriend. And he lay next to me and let me have my cries on the boat that night five years ago, and many nights after.

Music and clapping erupted from the TV, and psychic medium John Edward walked forward.

"Ooh! Crossing Over is on!" I said. I never had time for John Edward anymore—or Oprah who was right after him—only on vacation and sick days. We got here just in time for him to stand on the lit-up circular white stage as if stepping onto a cloud, scope out the audience, and begin his readings.

"She tells me you have something of hers that you're wearing," John said to the first woman in the audience he tuned into. "She shows me you clutching."

"Yes. I'm always wearing a locket of my sister's," said the woman, "and I always carry her picture inside and I'm always holding on to her."

Mom moved to the couch and squeezed on the other side of my thighs.

Conor sipped his drink and looked out at the harbor. He showed his disbelief with silence, like my friend Anne at work any time I brought up a cool John Edward reading on our lunch time walks. It was hard not to take it personally. Mom had a sixth sense—*ESP*, she called it. She *just knew* things: who's calling when the kitchen phone didn't have caller ID, that Dad's car was stolen from its parking spot as they swayed on the dance floor as newlyweds, that an old friend was in Boston as she drove through the tunnel under his hotel. And Mom had been one to consult with a psychic or two, because her talent was like an untamable husky; she could never predict her own life or anyone else's on command. Her destiny was this, a good local psychic named Ada had said: *You will end up with a guy who's surrounded by water.* And then Bill appeared at the Ivanhoe, her favorite Thursday night restaurant and bar. Bill with his island cabin on a lake in the southern end of the Berkshires. Bill with his accounting business in the foothills that would become our home.

Too bad Ada had crossed over. What I would *give* for someone like that to bring Gret through and tell me something only she'd know; show me that she had truly landed in a "better place" after all the collapses on arthritic bones and circle-walking. That the real her had survived the injection of sodium pentobarbital as I held her other paw at the foot of Mom's bed. I searched mediums online and found someone on the Cape near where I did my Tufts graduate work, but chickened out. I wasn't about to tell Conor I was going to a psychic—plus it was *a lot* of money.

"I thought of poor Gret this morning." Mom said during a commercial, holding my arm and dropping a machine gun round of little kisses on my head as I kept my gaze on the screen.

"Oh she's good and she knows she's good!" Mom sang her little sing-song for Gret, which got me to smile just a little.

"Poor Chickie-Dee."

I thought of Gret nonstop, for *five years*. I breathed in a belly full of salt air and let it out, and took a swig. It had kind of been five years of hell. More. I'd been working for animals ever since her fur had begun to lighten and there was only the *idea* of her dying, since my time at the animal hospital. But helping one suffering animal at a time on a clinic table was not enough; Talking with one owner of a suffering animal—like the college girl whose gecko had fallen into a coma on a New England winter day because of an improper tank setup—was not enough. My later job at the shelter Gretchen came from—an open-admission one with the constant parading in of animals and nonexistent spay/neuter clinic—and fundraising that brought in just enough to keep the status quo was definitely not enough.

A humane education job would be enough: focus on that teaching bit that would prevent the saddest things I saw in all those places and even in the barns and labs at UMass, because HSUS worked *for all animals*, our tagline said. The whole country's youth was my audience now. I had a boss who believed in me and put me at ease; my words flowed easily with him. Then there was our brand-new president, a master of strategy and compassion who was going to expand our work for farm animals—just what I'd been waiting for. All of that would be enough for Gretchen's memory.

All of that was clear to me as the breeze swayed the Last Call between the tight bounds of its dock. What wasn't clear was that I was burying myself in work—not just for Gretchen's memory, but to bury the grief of her loss. Like my sister Cookie dug the grave for her dog Rascal—dug, dug, more than she needed to, huge shovels full, her face disfigured with grief. She had made the earth her grief and was on the attack. I was on the attack for precision and quantity as I climbed the ranks of animal protection. But no amount of shoveling or strategizing behind a desk was enough to slay the beast of grief. It was just better than lying down and bawling.

Top: A visit to Nana's house, c· 1996; Bottom: Hanging out in Mom's room in Southwick, 1999

2

Girl Clothes Are the Cutest

The wooden OPEN sign hung by the picture window of Scarlet Begonia, the best shop on Block Island. Strings of colorful knitted fish dangled in the breeze against a propped-open door.

My sister, Nellie, went straight for the Silpada jewelry at the far end of the counter, navigating silver necklaces through her wavy, sun-brightened hair, pulling her long fingers down over pendants laid out on her tan chest. Mom surveyed yellow and purple oversized cotton beach clothes, screeching hangers on metal rods. I went for the knick-knacks, which I already had too many of.

Amidst floral planters and Kleenex box covers, a rack of baby dresses pulled at me.

"Ooooooh!" I said, sucking in air. "A cat and dog dress!"

They weren't just any cats and dogs. They were the old-fashioned ones, The Three Little Kittens Golden Book kind. Repeated scenes of them: Kittens and puppies sleeping. Kittens playing with yarn. Kittens and puppies sitting there and looking cute. A cat face stitched in red on the front pocket of the pale yellow cotton, mouth, and whiskers just like I drew them as a kid. My uterus thumped along with my heart, and visions flashed through my mind: of my first dolls wearing dresses like that; of feeding my baby cousin a bottle at age 6 or 7, the sucking motion of her mouth; of the infant I babysat when I was 17, when I really started wanting one of my own.

I twisted the hanger, making the dress catch the air and reveal matching bloomers underneath, and pictured my future baby spinning in it without a care, picking dandelions, like I used to. I was going to have a baby—a little girl, I was sure. And it would be the best thing I ever did—well, *one* of the best things.

"Oh, Chick," Mom said, coming over. "That's adorable!"

"You're going to have one, Chickie." She got louder and looked me in the eye.

"You have to get it."

"Maybe I will," I said. A smile formed as I turned to Mom's ear. "You know, I even thought of a name?"

"You did?" Mom said.

"Yup," I said.

The smile grew.

"Lauren Patricia," I whispered.

I had been through a bunch of combinations since I was 19 years old. Gretchen Lauren. Lauren Gretchen. Lauren, I just liked. Patricia is Mom's first name.

"Oh, Chickie! You don't have to do that!"

"No—I want to! I *like* it."

She took the dress and studied it proudly. "Well I love it. Very classy. Oh, look at the cute little bloomers! BLOO-MARZ!" Mom said it Nana-style.

"BLOO-MARZ!" I joined in before snatching it off the rack like I'd pulled Gretchen's cage card on her adoption day.

Oh, my Gretchen! I thought. The triangle note thrown in her grave flashed through my mind. *How many times did I envision this dream of a baby, and she was by my side?* I pictured her lounging on her side while I changed my Cabbage Patch Kid, Yetti Lynn's diaper.

Where was she, right at this second? How *was she?*

"Whatcha gettin Heid?" Nellie asked.

I picked up the hanger I'd just clanked down on the desk and held it up.

"Awww," she said. "So does this mean you're really trying?"

"Kind of!" I said, "We're laying the groundwork."

Truth was, I couldn't wait any longer. After hemming and hawing with Conor for years about right timing, the feeling had hit me in my center one day, like when I'd first laid eyes on Gretchen and just knew.

I *needed* a baby.

"Well, that groundwork better involve some action," she said, slamming her hand in the other palm. "You saw the hell I went through to have mine."

Nellie and Gabe were years older than me and Conor, and modern medicine helped them bring little Jackson and Sabrina into the world. I'd heard Nellie spill enough jargon on in vitro and insemination, fertility and aging, for the past, oh, eight years to remind me that I wasn't getting any younger. I'd be 30 in eight months.

Conor and I had started laying the groundwork. I'd talked with the doctor and taken her advice to get medication out of my system. We paid attention to couple time, since that would be hard to come by with a baby, and took a trip to Ireland last April. We went to extra lengths to prove ourselves at work, because lack of sleep and maternity time and all that would cramp our work style— if I kept my job. I always pictured an idyllic home life with a baby spent lolling in a carpeted family room next to a kitchen full of brightly-colored sippy cups. I also thought I'd save the country's animals. I never thought about how both would play together.

Nellie was right. We needed to make it happen. I also needed to make hay with work *until* it happened. The San Diego workshops were coming up. I'd just started the Toastmasters meetings in Springfield to improve my speaking skills, to do better for Gretchen and all animals before relaxing at home with soon-to-come baby Lauren for a while.

But first, I would have a little fun.

I was in Block Island.

You could always walk into a packed tourist destination with Mom, and a parking spot or the right number of bar stools would appear.

Mom confidently led the way to a newly-vacant corner table in front of Walter, the Irish folksinger at the Mahogany Shoals bar. Mahogany Shoals was in a little barn of an outbuilding right on Payne's Dock, just steps from the Last Call.

"Way hay and up she rises!" Mom belted out with her signature smile. "Way hay and up she rises! Way hay and up she rises early in the marning!"

Feet stomped the wooden floor that matched the docks, but Walter's wiry Irish Wolfhound lay comatose at his feet. I chimed in, tapping the wobbly table with my fist, and smiled into Nana's eyes glinting in the glow of the string lights. This song always came on the Irish station in her kitchen on weekend mornings as she cooked. Nana was the best: a confidante and dream-sharer and friend. On our mall outing for my birthday last March, I had fawned over a little pink zip-up sweatshirt that matched mine at Children's Place. When we got to the car, she pulled out a bright-striped box that held the tiny sweatshirt and pink booties to match. *Just put it away, Chickie,* she whispered in her adorable high-pitched voice. It was Nana's and my secret, like Lauren Patricia was with Mom.

"Tied up with a black velvet band!" Mom's eyes squinted at the next song, her Sambuca held high with three coffee beans for health, wealth, and happiness. I yawned, but we'd stay until the last drop was gone. The ice swayed in the snifter like the boat rocked me to bed.

The sun coming in through the skylight of the V-berth in the boat's bow woke me before Conor or anyone. I slid off the triangular mattress, threw my clothes on, and snuck around Nellie and the kids strewn over the pull-out coach, stepped gently onto the dock and past the hibachi grills on the sidewalk.

In the take-out line amidst the sugary air of Payne's "killer donut" stand, behind girls punching in numbers at the register, it was there: the life-size photo of this dock and people coming and going with their fishing poles and scooters. Only the scooters weren't so bright and modern. *Payne's Dock 1984* was hand-painted at the bottom. A year before Gretchen came into the world and into my life.

This was where I stood five years ago and thought, *There was another time, when Gretchen wasn't here. And life went on.*

That pre-Gretchen photo of Payne's was the one thing that brought me comfort that first, raw week after her passing. It helped me step away with my bags of donuts with more lightness in my steps, into a future that wasn't what I wanted, but was possible. It wasn't hard to get to the work Gretchen had led me to and get lost in the to-do lists and pressure of the nonprofit world.

But a baby? A baby was a whole different thing.

A baby was joy that touched a spot that was Gretchen's.

When I attended my first Animal Care Expo for sheltering and rescue professionals, I sat in workshops headed by sociologists and psychologists, fascinated to learn more about animal-human relationships.

"How many of you are only children or the youngest child in your family?" one presenter asked, a PhD in sociology.

I raised my hand, and began to look around me. Everyone's hand was up.

None of us had younger siblings to take care of. In their absence, it was theorized, we'd moved to others who needed care and protection.

Was it why I loved my first puppy, Oliver, so much? Why I took losing him so hard?

Was it why I spent my childhood free time caring for field mice and eggs fallen from trees?

I was a nurturer. No, a *supernurturer*, the presenter said. I guess I was super for going above and beyond most people's definition of caring for others because of my pent-up need for it. If I were to put in layman's terms, I had a bright red thumping heart with a clear view out to the world's littlest creatures in need. I mean, I named a field mouse and made cheese deliveries.

But like Oliver, Speedy didn't stick around too long.

Gretchen did. She was the living, breathing, object of all my capacity for love and caring, stored up in my bright red thumping heart.

You really loved that dog, Bill would say.

Mom said I never gave her one day of trouble. That's how Gret was. She was an observer and thinker like me. She was one of those rare friends you could sit next to doing absolutely nothing and be completely at ease. There was a quiet peace and understanding in the space between us where my red heart was free to beat the loudest.

That dog made me who I am. Nothing and no one would take her place.

As much as my body yearned for a baby, there was something deeper—19 years deeper—that pushed back.

My loyalty to Gretchen.

Dear Gretchen

- I always had an affinity for animals and desire to help, but two individuals came into my life and helped significantly. One is a dog. Gretchen - my dog of 14 years — passed away in '99 — it's emotional — I'll try to get thru this.
- Like a sister — there for me — having her as a friend helped me build empathy — I wanted to help animals like her.
- She was brought from RI from a neighbor & friend of a friend who lived 1 street away— shelter brought us together (We missed each other when she was in my neighborhood the 1st time).
- The universe was trying to unite us.

Notes from my First Speech at Toastmaster's International Induction Ceremony, 6/14/04

Dear Gretchen

3

A Walk to Wagner

The gurgle of the water always stilled me if I stood long enough, and let deep thoughts meander out like water between the rocks. The youth education division of The Humane Society of the United States was on a crook of the Eightmile River in East Haddam, Connecticut, in the log cabin across the road from the bridge I stood on. A forties Broadway actress loved the area, and had the cabin built as a teaching center three years after America celebrated its first Earth Day. *This* was the place to teach kids about wildlife and their habitats, with the watershed and deer and otters and snakes. Inside the cabin was a big room designed for lessons on pet care. I could picture bright-eyed children filing in off school busses from Hartford or New London into the circular drive, falling under the trance of this river and exploring the 30-acres of trails.

By the time I had gotten the job last year, in 2003, a lot had changed. The trails had grown over. Instead of leading nature walks we pecked at our keyboards like the wild turkeys, spreading our work more evenly over the whole country. Our classroom newspaper, *KIND News**, went to 34,000 classrooms, about a million sets of bright eyes. My job was to market our materials in every way possible: through ads and articles and promotional emails and trade show booths and Powerpoint presentations, often juggling multiple computer screens.

I held out my right arm, palm down, then up, stretching my wrist from overworking the computer mouse.

"River's low," Cathy said, bellying up to the railing next to me over the river, the breeze ruffling a lock of her perfectly-cut caramel hair.

Cathy was my office neighbor who had written for *KIND News* since her kids were grown. She had a Golden Retriever named Jesse who liked to fetch a ball from the same Berkshires lake as the one my stepfather, Bill's island cottage sat on.

"Yeah," I said, fluffing the front of my shirt. "must be this *heat*."

"Lorie's coming."

I crouched down in a hamstring stretch for our daily lunchtime power walk, and felt the dull ache in my right ankle from keeping my foot on the gas pedal for my long commute.

Our office manager Lorie descended from the cabin's side door pushing an odd-looking, screen-covered baby carriage. She was careful not to let the thing escape down

---

* Kind News is now published by RedRover, KindNews.org.

the circular drive as she checked in on her cargo: a brown tabby cat.

I was not the only supernurturer at the cabin.

The cat had sprung up onto our boss Ed's window screen one day. As an office, we practiced what we preached about responsible pet care, posting flyers within five miles. When no owner turned up, no one could say no to *Ginger*. Lorie wasted no time in naming her and stepping up to be Ginger's person. She would handle her vet care and weekend care. During the week, Ginger was free to roam the offices, rubbing on our legs and jumping on our backs without warning, perching like a parrot as we pecked at the keys.

"*That's* the new cat stroller?" I asked, still stretching my ankle. "It looks like one of those old prams like from Mary Poppins!"

"I know!" Lorie laughed, "Let's see how she likes it."

We set off, Lorie wheeling Ginger ahead of us, and Cathy and I sped up to peek in. Ginger looked up through the screen at the full green canopy of the forest from which she came, hers to wander no more. There were Eastern coyotes out there, for sure, and bobcats and raccoons. So many fights just waiting for her, not to mention sports car drivers putting their handling to the test on our winding road.

"So the San Diego workshops were good?" Lorie asked my way.

"*Very*," I said, dropping my head for emphasis. "We had like 40 people." I thought of my confidence with the animal control officers and shelter caregivers from all around Southern California, my voice projecting better, the hands raised for questions at the end. Toastmasters had started working already, and I'd done it. I'd connected with them.

"And Helen Woodward Animal Center was incredible. They have a therapeutic riding ring, a pet boarding resort, and there were like three youth camp groups going on the morning we were there. And Mike Arms was so cool," I said, thinking about the center's president. "Told me his whole story. He was totally burned out in his first shelter job in New York and put in his resignation. In his last week, he got a call that a puppy was hit by a car and broke his back. He got to the scene of the accident and two bystanders told him not to take the dog; they were taking bets on how long "it" was going to live. He bent down to lift the puppy into the ambulance, and they attacked him with a bat and a knife, knocking him out. Mike said the dog shouldn't have been able to move, but crawled to him and licked his face til he came to. At that moment he basically asked God if he let him live, he'd do everything to protect animals. And now he's saving millions with these genius adoption campaigns."

A little BMW convertible whizzed toward us on the blind side of the curve. I picked up my pace and led the way to the other side.

"So did the puppy live?" Lorie asked.

"No," I said, trudging forward.

Like Mike, I knew what it was like to be driven by one special animal.

I also knew burnout, the kind caused by suffering and death.

My previous job at the shelter had focused on coordinating special projects, mainly the annual Walk for Animals—our biggest fundraiser that I had taken Gretchen back for in our Southwick years when I volunteered there. What better way to honor her memory than to make it my full-time job to run the thing and put my all into it?

But it hadn't been all ordering T-shirts, securing sponsorships and police details, and training volunteers from my office above the shelter. I'd gone downstairs to help with the animals long enough. With 10,000 animals a year squeezing through the glass doors and less than half walking out, I'd entered a new world in the same city as the animal hospital I'd started out in—one of too many animals and not enough people to own them.

At every turn of my shelter work I looked for Gretchen in other dogs, but only found a deepening of the wounds from losing her. There had been the older shepherd mix, Celia, who had Gretchen's shape and quiet demeanor, who I'd adopted out to the nicest mom and little girl, who quickly brought her back for peeing in the house. I'd left a check to cover Celia's spay surgery before leaving for Block Island that year. *That'll help her peeing problem,* I thought. *That'll get her adopted for good.* I came back to find out that Celia developed a lameness and was euthanized while I walked State Beach.

And unlike in my childhood shelter visits and college volunteer days, I had been allowed—*needed* in the last place you want to be in a shelter, the area for Personnel Only: the second to the last room before the back door, that I'd first learned about from my brother Rocky when I was nine on one of our Saturday shelter visits.

"You know what happens behind that door, don't you," young Rocky had stated more as a fact than a question as he casually read cage cards, looking all Miami Vice with his brown hair fluffy on top, hitting the collar of his graphic print Hawaiian-style shirt in the back. I had been crouched down, peering in at one of the poor helpless souls—a lanky hound mix taking up most of his metal walls—thinking how I'd come in and walk him. I'd walk all of them. They'd just have to pay me $2 an hour. What did I know about volunteers doing it for free?

Rocky looked back at me and swiped four straight fingers across his neck.

I looked around—at the exposed pipes in the ceiling that seemed to have gone beneath me, the cement floor above me. The door marked "Personnel Only." And the air began to go away.

Fifteen years later, I'd gone behind the door. I'd lived that too-terrible-to-believe reality.

They were the bouncing young shepherd mixes said to be carriers of Parvovirus, a contagious and fatal virus of the intestines. The flashbacks came hard: The slow aiming of the needle. The requisite flash of red. The blue that ends lives.

It's hard to say what happened to my heart that day at the shelter. I couldn't look at the damage right away. The me I always knew couldn't handle it, so she went away. I still ordered the T-shirts and booked the police detail and helped in the cat room, but I was some kind of ghost floating through the lobby and down the cinderblock halls. The old me was who-knows-where.

"I think she likes it!" Cathy said, following my gaze into Ginger's carriage.

The road straightened out and I quickened my pace enough to see her, lying on her little tuffet behind the screen with her little front paws tucked under her, sniffing at the forest air. She looked up at me, then back to the woods.

"There he is!" Cathy and Lorie squealed in unison.

I looked ahead on yet another bend of our country road to see the silhouette of the stocky black lab that is Wagner, slowly pulling himself off his driveway.

His tail wagged low and slow, propelling his thick body and smiling face to us.

I caught up to find Cathy down on her knees.

"Ah sa good boy Wagner!" she beamed.

I'd never heard such volume in Cathy's voice than in her daily, weekday reunion with Wagner.

Lorie parked Ginger at the driveway's end to get her dog fix before offering a Milk Bone from her cat-braceleted hand, which made Wagner's rump shake even harder.

I hovered over the scene.

I should be in there. The words came faintly as they high-talked and ear-scratched, *like them.* But I couldn't move. I'd already faked it so many times, but I just wanted, just for once, for it to come on its own.

Lorie started to fix her pony tail and look back to our route, so I pushed myself over.

"Hi Wagner," I said as flat as a pancake.

Could he even hear me? Could *they*? I felt myself squat and watched my hand extend toward him, palm-down as I'd been teaching in my workshops. He licked it, a slobbery, crumby Milk-Bone lick, and I saw the white hairs poking out of his muzzle—just like Gretchen's at the end—and pulled back, nearly toppling over. I recovered, gave a quick pat to his head, and mixed back into my group, back to the road.

I just wanted to help dogs. I wanted to love them.

And now it hurt.

It was easy to bury myself in the business side of it.

It was easy to think that dogs like Wagner didn't need me. Only animals in trouble did.

But man did I miss greeting a strange dog on a street corner. I used to squeal with delight like Cathy and Lorie. I used to tend to my bright red thumping heart which no longer had a clear view on the world. It was pale. Quiet. Calloused.

When did it all change? It was at the animal hospital, in my first role bearing suffering and death on a daily basis.

"I feel myself changing," I had told Leslie, another vet tech, as we dangled our legs from the pharmacy counter in the quiet late hours of the 3-11 shift.

Emotional changes are subtle and creeping like a mole on your skin changes form. Only it's not easy to ask someone to check on your emotional state like you can a dot on your skin.

I had come into that job with that thumping red heart, like the sparkly-eyed Buddha setting out into a world of suffering from the gates of his palace, eager to see what he could see and learn. And what I saw changed me within months: the "stat" call during a thunderstorm that pulled me to the reception area where a Doberman pinscher lay dead from a heart attack. That poor comatose gecko.

That jolting feeling that went through my body, that shock and sadness trying to find its way out, began to eerily disappear.

Like everything else, I was quiet about it, and good thing; I'd seen my share of looks about anyone going desensitized. Anyway, it's not like anyone had known of anything that could be done about it. And we weren't there to talk about our feelings; we had clients to get in and out and medicine to dispense.

"It happens to everyone," Leslie replied before jumping down and sitting cross-legged on the hall floor between two exam rooms. Maybe Leslie's trauma went inward. Twice I found her at that spot on the floor, doubled over with stomach cramps she had casually shrugged off as "IBS"—Irritable Bowel Syndrome. The new vet, Crystal, had had no problem letting it out; I found her in the same position outside the x-ray room bawling after a cat's owners couldn't afford surgery to remove curling ribbon he'd eaten, and had elected for euthanasia. Crystal was the nicest, always looking you in the eye with a smile. She had jumped into this big ole pot of suffering and death as excited and wide-eyed as me, looking to love every animal in front of her like a childhood pet.

But I didn't cry or protest with a chronic illness. I just thought, *So this is how it is*, and let the suffering and death sink deep, to the best part of me: my red, thumping, heart. I'd later learn at the conferences that this phenomenon had a name: *compassion fatigue*, exhaustion from suffering and death tied to caring professions.

A bluejay squawked, and I realized I was letting Cathy and Lorie hold the conversation for the three of us. But they would never understand what was going on in my head. They had bypassed the hospitals and shelters and went straight for the office jobs.

I noticed the rhythm of my feet again, and the woods cushioning the river came into focus. The sun was sneaking through from above the canopy, finding its way toward me, moving as the breeze moved the leaves. As its rays bent, they turned a reddish hue. A picture of the rainbow I saw in Ireland last April flashed through my mind; the sign I had asked my late Papa for on one commute home before the trip. I was going to the same places where he'd taken me months before he died. *Maybe you could show me a sign there; show me you're with me on this trip, too.* And where the highway bends east on its way up to Springfield, a rainbow had appeared to the west.

I had quietly looked for that rainbow on every coach ride and every sightseeing stop of our Southern Ireland tour. Conor hadn't known why I was looking off into the countryside as we strolled through a castle, why I'd surveyed the sky above the sea from the Cliffs of Moher. And when we window-shopped in Killarney—in a town Papa had taken me and Nana on a jaunting cart from, around the lakes, in 1988—when I'd forgotten about the rainbow for a minute, Conor stopped me mid-driveway between two buildings, and pointed above a rutted parking lot to Papa's rainbow.

The cabin came into sight, and I realized I was smiling like my Irish eyes were in the spring. That's what I needed! A sign from Gretchen, because maybe she could still be with me, too. Maybe then I'd know she was OK, and then I could breathe again.

Maybe then I could heal my heart.

Dear Gretchen

4

Flower Power

I squeaked the door open and was hit with the signature smell of my workplace. We may have gotten weekly W.B. Mason deliveries and stored our meeting minutes in file cabinets like any office in corporate America, but ours had walls made of stacked logs and smelled of Bill's island cabin: of damp earth and wood.

The wide pine floors gave a creak on my first step and right away, our benefactors' eyes were on me. The doe-eyed portrait of the 40s actress who had the place built presided above the big stone fireplace of the big room. She was one of the first to welcome me here six years earlier, and watched close as I delivered my presentation on coyotes in children's literature alongside my Tufts mentor.

I made my way down the hall, past our tiny kitchen and bathrooms, to my office at the end. The little cut-out of my picture from the annual report on my mailbox, a screenshot from my interview on dog bite prevention on NBC's John Walsh Show, still stuck there from an anonymous office friend.

"Morning!" I shouted from the hall to Cathy as my iced coffee made waves in the cup.

Cathy was my across-the-hall neighbor, but our doors practically touched.

"Morning!" she said. "We're going to the herb farm today!"

"Oh!" I shouted back as I turned on the computer tower, dropped my purse, and waited for my screens to appear.

Cathy walked in as I gave my silent weekday morning "hello" to Gretchen with her Giants football in the little metal dog frame. She had squinted in full sun on the lush, flat lawn as wide as Mom's sprawling ranch, framed by tall arborvitaes and woods.

"Have you been, in Salem?" Cathy asked.
"No."

"You're going to love it!" she says. "Lorie and I have done our planting. We're just going for fun. They have some beautiful decorative stuff and gifts, and the grounds are gorgeous."

It was Friday, and I was in great shape. I had gotten the proof of our Programs & Materials Catalog yesterday and the only thing on my morning calendar was to make sure the designer made all the last edits I'd sent, and have him send the final file for the printer.

"Oh, fun," I said. "I'll go. I even brought my lunch today."

At noon sharp, I stepped onto the creaking big room floor to find Lorie, and we descended the wide front porch to Cathy's car, A/C already blasting.

"This is nice!" I said. "To be driven for a change. Maybe I'll find a plant for our back deck at home that I've done nothing with since we moved in."

An angel weathervane glinted in the sun above the sign when we arrived.

Salem Herbfarm

Open daily 9-5 – Herbs – Perennials – Pansies

A painted-on rooster and hen played below the words as we paraded through an opening in a stone wall. The wall went way back and encircled a maze-like English country garden.

After we parked, I stepped over a running hose that reminded me of carefree summer days of youth. The air weighed on my skin. A buffet of sights was there for sampling: a fiesta of plant life in reds, oranges, and purples. Sparrows bobbed down to birdbaths, the most adorable weathered vintage metal ones—each with the statue of a bird already sitting in them. A mansion of a bird house perched on a pole in the center of the maze. Gazebos made of twisting branches centered their own flower beds of daisies, in lush swaths. Happy flowers. Mom's favorites.

A huge barn housed the shop. Potted plants dotting the wide porch sucked me in. Each one, its own little perfectly-coordinated garden: rosemary, spearmint, lemon thyme, alpine strawberry. Plants had never pleased me so much. It was as if each leaf bending in the breeze whispered: *There's life outside of work to keep animals alive.* And when the breeze stilled: *We're perfectly happy, just sitting here in the summer air.*

Inside was a wall of glazed pottery pots—one for me. And a wall of the little vintage birdbaths—one for Mom.

I stood in line, balancing the tiny garden and pot and mini birdbath I'd chosen, and the seed packets standing up at the register caught my eye.

WILDFLOWERS.

Commit random acts of kindness and senseless acts of beauty.

Beautiful indeed: The picture below the words on the package showed yellows, reds, blues, shooting up this way and that. Random. Wildflowers sprouted when and where they wanted, between rocks or alongside highways, accepting whatever rain and animal poo nature provides as sustenance.

I balanced my loot on the checkout counter, and grabbed a packet, the seeds shaking in the thin space of the paper. A shake of these seeds above ground could be a wish. Their sprouts, my answer. It made all the sense in the world. The wooded part of my yard with all its still wisdom was where I went to feel closer to Gretchen. It was a place for consolation akin to Mom's bedside when I'd been sick in the night. I could drop the tiny seeds there and ask Gretchen to make a bloom, to show her safety and soundness. She could do that now that she's a spirit. She could do anything, couldn't she?

At 5:00, I grabbed my flowers from the cabin porch and set out for my little green Honda. I stashed my Herb Farm loot in the trunk, pulled onto on our country road, and hit the button on the sunroof to let the breeze pour in. The car was dependable and fun, with bells and whistles that came free with cars purchased slightly used.

A commercial buzzed on the radio. Rush hour was the worst. I hit the button for the 10-CD changer in the trunk. I thought of the discs that went with the different slot numbers in the line-up in my trunk. #1: I liked Michelle Branch, but was getting sick of that one. #2: Aaliyah always reminded me of my shelter days, of one of the staff, Vinnie, dancing in the back of his pickup at a Forest Park event for the dogs. #3: JAY-Z was best for a drive through the city. #4 and 5: Ah, a good ole classic, the perfect background music to my homeward-bound dreams of Gretchen—the 2-disk *Mariah Carey Greatest Hits*.

I did my evening scan of the open field beyond the stone wall for deer or wild turkeys or—cross fingers—a coyote. I knew it was Gretchen's look that had drawn me to coyotes, to studying and writing about them hour after hour at Tufts. Finally, the Native American burial ground

I only knew was there from a neighbor marked the end of the road.

A couple quick jogs, and I was on the first highway, the solitary, rock-flanked, 2-laner that is Route 11. This was where Pam in the mailroom hit a deer, sending the animal running and leaving her covered in bits of glass. I kept my hands at 10 and 2 and tried to relax my shoulders. Finding a lifeless dragonfly on my windshield was just as hard a hit for me, cancelling out animals this trip was supposed to help.

Route 11 merged into Route 2, a much busier highway separating the casinos and Rhode Island from home. "I Don't Wanna Cry" came on—the breakup song for Cookie and her old boyfriend—and I was in that brainless driving groove. My body knew every turn, every elevation change, every lane shift to get my little car onto Route 91, toward Springfield, when everything got brighter no matter the weather because I was almost home. And that's when the song came on.

"When You Believe" is a duet with Whitney Houston, from the *Prince of Egypt* Movie. I've heard Whitney Houston say that God spoke through her singing, and I could hear it now, with every breathy word, every confident declaration. She was speaking to me. God was speaking to me. Every line hit my core. And I replied.

There can *be miracles. I* do *believe. I* know *what miracles I can achieve. I* will. *I believe. The seeds can do it. Gretchen can do it.*

My exit off 91 wound past Barney Hill of Forest Park. I glanced through the scrub to catch my daily split-second view of the bottom of the hill where Nellie, Cookie, Rocky and I had wiped out as kids into the little half frozen brook, clutching one another's backs on Dad's toboggan on one of our Tuesday nights with him. Nana lived in the town next to the park, Longmeadow. And that's why I put up with this commute every day. To never be far from Nana or Mom on a Friday night or a Saturday or Sunday.

After a grid-locked trip across the South End Bridge, I gunned it onto the last highway: Route 57. Three exits to Garden Street. After living at the top of our first three-family home, Conor and I finally had a house to ourselves. Conor and Mom had found it while I was at the New England Federation of Humane Societies' Conference in Newport.

And they'd done good. It had a farmhouse front porch, cul-de-sac location, and a wooded backyard that abutted a Fish & Game Club. It was right on the highway to our jobs, and Mom's was in the next town west of us.

I pulled into the driveway and glided in just as the garage door rose above my hood. Conor's spot was empty: He was golfing in West Hartford with the guys from the office. I grabbed my purse and heard the *shake, shake, shake* of the seed packet.

I walked out back still in my trance, the song in my head, and stood on the ledge of grass before the ravine gave way to the craggy, wild part of our yard where nothing but piles of brown leaves grow, before the woods.

Please, Gretchen. Show me you're OK. Send up a flower as beautiful as your soul.

I tore the top of the packet open, held the bottom, and made one wide swoop with my hand. They promptly reported back with a *tap, tap, tap* on crisp leaves. Now the next rain could do its work, send them onto whatever soil lies beneath, where whatever streams of sunlight would reach. Whatever happened next, it was up to the universe, God, and Gretchen.

5

Running Back in Time

My clock went off early, and I slipped out of bed fast so as not to wake up Conor. I'd been telling myself I would try the new elliptical machine he got for the newly-finished basement for days and days, and finally decided to make it happen. I could never keep a gym membership going, but I knew this would be a good start to the day and help wake me up for my long drive.

I stepped on the pedals and futzed with the controls. Five on the RPE, whatever that meant. I grabbed the remote from the little TV tray table Conor had set up and punched the *on* button at the TV. Out came the melancholic whistle of the Scorpions lead singer. I never watched MTV anymore. It was MTV Classic; "Wind of Change" on some oldies show. Gretchen loved the wind; it always made her put her nose in the air and made her prance higher on our walks. I got going in an easy run and recalled a snapshot of her proud walk, nose up on someone's lawn across the street and around the bend from Mom's. Reaching the end of the side-street perpendicular to ours, I'd forget about the neighbors and unhook the leash. I'd stay on my street path, of course, turn onto Deer Run that ran parallel to our street, and turn my head at about the third driveway down. Gretchen would come barreling over the hill that was the front yards, making her own wind, straight to my outstretched hands, and I'd hook her back up again before the main road.

The sad, slow bass of "What's Up" By 4 Non Blondes started up. What a blast from the past! It used to come on my pink boom box while I studied on the front step at Mom's, Gretchen lying on the warm concrete next to me. The song sang of revolution, which brought to mind a revolt from modern ways and a return to an older, simpler lifestyle to save our environment. I'd been reading about it in the novel *Ishmael* for my prim English professor, Dr. Copeland, at Holyoke Community College. It was just one of the mind-opening stories with an animal as a main character that made me see that reading a book wasn't the worst thing, and could even make a difference.

Those were also the days of "sock game," of grabbing a pair that had seen better days from my drawer and using it as the object of some of the best games of fetch and tug-of-war I'd ever seen. I remembered slowly creeping into that top drawer as if it were a treat jar, shifty-eyed, slowly plucking a thready pair, and flinging it up across my bedroom. Gretchen would flip it up with her nose, chomp it and run, only slowing to tip-toe across the slippery parquet floor of the front entry hall. She'd pick up speed on the carpet of the sunken living room, and hide under the dining room table where she'd hunker down, sock between her paws, and pull at it with her tiny little front teeth. I'd drop down with her, find a scrap sticking out, and pull. "*My* sock!!!" She'd always let me get it, because she was a gentle dog, and because then the game could start again.

Holding a sock for Gretchen in Southwick, c. 1994
Maybe a game before class?

The elliptical machine came to a stop, but I stood still on the pedals, staring into nothing. The song still played, and I could almost still feel the sun-baked cement that we had sat on, ten years earlier, my book on my lap, Mom in the house with something on the stove.

On the road to work, I thought of what John Edward said about songs. *They can be signs from those on the Other Side.* I didn't need a psychic to connect us. We could do it, just the two of us. I thought of the seeds. I had no clue how much time a wildflower needed to germinate, find its way up through brown leaves, and make a flower to say hello to me. But I knew it had every ingredient it needed, and that miracles were possible. I just couldn't go out back after work and look that day, or the day after. I'd be patient, and one day, go out and find my prize.

It was easier said than done. When you're waiting for something you want with all your being, you turn another layer of ghostly, of one going through motions and drifting through a still world. Down time was the worst. On lunch breaks, you place your order at the restaurant and let your friends talk. You sit and watch life some more, in slow motion.

6

Help, Michael

Summer's days were shortening. Mornings, I'd drive out of the garage to find dew on the grass. Fog along the highway accumulated on my windshield.

Evenings were shortening, too.

I came home from work with an extra spring in my step that bonked the first board on the garage stairs into the kitchen. I dropped my purse and the day's action alerts from work on the breakfast bar—"armchair lobbyist" tasks from HQ that I'd do in a spare moment that never seemed to come.

I grabbed a can of Bud and watched the beams of westerly sun stream into the big picture window by our kitchen table. I wandered to the deck to watch the sun slink behind the woods. The strawberries and spearmint from the Herb Farm were doing well; the thyme and rosemary saw better days. I sat back and breathed deep toward the expanse of woods. A dragonfly landed at the top of the stairs; a visitor to the pond back there.

"We'd have to watch a baby close here," Conor had said sitting here on a lazy weekend last year. The stairway wound two stories down to the patio outside the walk-out basement. And that thought had brought us to a consensus: Watching a crawly baby is a lot of work. And we'd have this baby for the rest of our lives, so what's another year of quiet with our beers?

Now, my best friend Jessica planned my 30th birthday, which would fall on a Friday.

"Make sure you take the day off," she had said.

Jessica was great when it came to celebrations. This year, we were both going to pamper ourselves: makeup at the Filene's Origins counter. Hair at Gasoline Alley with Paul, my aunt's brother. License renewal for me, at the same Registry I accompanied Jessica at for her first driver's license.

And now, we were just about ready for a child. This very house, we picked with a child in mind. The cul-de-sac. The kitchen open to the family room so we could watch a baby as we cooked and washed sippy cups.

I felt the beer fizzling its way to my brain.

And thoughts of Gretchen came, sweet Gretchen, the dog I really didn't want to take this step without. And she would show me I didn't have to. That she was listening and alive not just in memory but in spirit. She would show her presence, with a bloom as beautiful as she was—*is*.

It was time.

A smile formed in my lips and I stood up and aimed it toward the woods.

I descended the two-story stairs, slowly, as if hesitating would give a bloom more time to open. I crossed the narrow strip of grass and the swail that separated the cultivated from the wild part of our yard, down into the ravine and looked for solid footing. I stood and scanned the brown scrub for...purple? Yellow? Red? I would accept any one of them.

When my eyes turned up nothing, I started toeing the ground, then kicking.

Nothing. Just brown leaves and a nip bottle with the label worn off.

I lifted my gaze up toward the fish & game club and expanded my visual search, and found a vast floor of brown peppered by the green leaves of saplings. A lone crow's caw echoed off the crisp leaves lining the forest floor.

The sun was blocked now, the sky overcast. I couldn't stand to think of my dog as dead. Yet there I was, my head hung above lifeless leaves where new life was supposed to be.

I heard the garage door opener jolt on, and straightened up. Conor.

I crunched my feet. I should have dinner going.

"Want to watch the Sopranos I recorded?" Conor asked as he sprayed down the sink.

"I'm too tired," I said. "Sorry. I need to go up."

I climbed the stairs and was greeted by Michael, my childhood teddy bear. I'd found him when I sealed away the Children's Place box from Nana. I picked him off the decorative pillows, turned down the bed, and pulled him close, melting his softness into me. It somehow, for a moment, filled the loneliness and longing.

How many times had I squeezed him for my first lost dog? For my lost home as a kid? How could a stuffed animal still do that to you at 29 and a half?

Why won't you show me? I asked the air, and held Michael tighter.

It wasn't the first time she didn't answer me. I'd gone wandering back in Mom's yard, too, shortly after her death, aimless, past the grave, looking for a sign. A different song had played in my head back then. The BeeGees. "How deep is your love?" It had been a sad playing, as if I asked the question to a spirit who flitted to me, then away too quickly. I hadn't been ready to think of her that way. I just wanted a mortal I could touch and keep tabs on like I always had.

I cried and squeezed some more, until the frogs between us and the fish & game club lulled me out of my misery.

7

Too Much Craziness

Route 91 was a parking lot approaching Hartford. That lightness in traffic that comes with prime summer vacation time was no more. And it was Friday.

Why was traffic always worse on Fridays?

People were definitely in a better mood. It was always my day to follow up with reporters, and Mia at Headquarters agreed. And apparently, being happy made people feel freer and more invincible to police. The single-driver vehicles had been caught red-handed trying to use the commuter lane, and now lined up, engines off, in the strip between the diamond lane and the rest of traffic.

It was a good time to check in with Mom.

"Hi Chick,"

I pictured her sitting by the old wall phone in the kitchen, but stopped myself from saying *How'd you know it's me?* It didn't take a psychic to know from her voice that something was wrong. The usual pep was gone.

"What's up Mom?"

"Oh, nothing," she said, before going quiet. Mom was never quiet. "It's just, Winnie won't answer her phone. I've been on with Danny since 7."

Poor Danny. Winnie's husband was sitting home with their new baby girl, alone. He couldn't reach her, either.

"What's going on with her?" I asked.

"Oh, Chickie," she said quickly, "It's just too much craziness to even get into."

I knew that Mom had been talking to her more than usual. She had cancelled appointments because she needed her. Mom was the go-to in the family when something was wrong. She wasn't a psychologist, but she listened like one. She was the one to go to. Mom got on her hands and knees with other peoples' problems. Illness. Money problems. Legal problems.

"Any scoops?" Mom asked as if she were stepping into a new room. "Any need for that little cat dress?"

"No Mom!" I shot back. "I will let you know when anything happens, I promise. No, right now I just have a lot going on at work."

"Well don't forget what Nellie went through, Chick," Mom warned. "I just know you want a little Lauren Patricia and you can't wait too long to have your little kitten."

Little Kitten, so cute, what Nana's been calling Mom since she was born. Nana always emphasized the *t*s when she said it.

"I'll be over soon, Mom." I said, "I have the Pet Rock promotion in Worcester tonight—you know they're sponsoring *KIND News*—and lunch with Ronnie tomorrow but I'll come Sunday."

"Ronnie" was starting to roll off the tongue. My prim English professor from community college was also an adjunct professor for the program of my dreams at Tufts. She became my mentor there, and then a friend. "Dr. Copeland" was now "Ronnie." I looked forward to our regular lunch meetings talking about animals and literature and careers.

"OK Chick," Mom said. "Tell Ronnie I said Hello."

"I will, Mama." I said. "Love ya."

"Love ya Chick."

I hung up and thought of Mom and her empty house and her worrying. If only Mom would pray for Winnie like Nana did; do something positive instead of talking about the negative things and thinking bad thoughts all the time. I had added her to my prayers at night on top of the usual "God bless Winnie" like Nana taught me. I added an extra one. *God help her find peace.* And an extra one for Mom. *God help her stop worrying so much. Help us all with our worry. Just help Winnie find peace and get on with her life.*

If only I was there to help talk Mom through things like I used to be. She hated when I had never moved back home after a year away at Tufts. I bought my first house and went straight there. She and Dad had always said I was a pleasure to be around. Like Gretchen. And now Mom was without both of us. Poor Mom. I had been so caught up in my career and houses, I never thought of her coming home from Block Island five years ago to pack up her bed and bowls and then walk by the site of them every day. I never thought of her stirring her coffee and looking through the criss-cross grates of the kitchen window to the wood pile Gret lay buried behind.

The thought of the letter in the ground jabbed at me. I wrote the words and protected them with all that tape. Gret had to know those words now. Spirits know everything.

Traffic picked up, and I turned back to the music. Would Gretchen's songs come on? There was "Runnin' Down a Dream" by Tom Petty. "Born To Be Wild" by Steppenwolf. I hit the scan button and waited. Nothing. It's OK. I had my own song now, that played on demand.

Disc number 5, track 9. "When You Believe" by Mariah Carey and Whitney Houston. And when it ended, I hit the back button and started it over, again, and again. Maybe Gret wasn't going to give me any sign. Maybe she was brushing me off, like the time I came back from a hospitalization. She was mad at me for leaving. Was she mad at me for ending her life? Because maybe I'd done that too early.

I would still ask for a miracle. I'd still play the song.

I played the song until the Native American burial ground on our country road welcomed me, and the river appeared through my passenger window, then the cabin in my windshield.

Dear Gretchen

8

There Can Be Miracles

It was a lazy Sunday. I woke up late, dragged myself downstairs, put the coffee on, and spread the Sunday Republican over half the kitchen table. I pushed down everything bagels and glimpsed the cats stretched out, absorbing a sunbeam that angled in through the tall front windows. One by one, I knelt down and ran my fingers down their backs, and heard the A/C crank on; the summer air had returned.

When the cool air jolted on again, the clock approached noon. I downed my coffee, ran up to find the closest shorts and T-shirt, and plunked down in the Honda. One push of the garage door button, and one of the sunroof, and *I* was absorbing rays and letting the humid air sink in to my skin. In New England, a later return of summer weather was a gift. It wouldn't last long.

I saw the Stop & Shop sign, swerved in, and found a spot near the entrance by the floral section. I scanned the refrigerated unit for the white and yellow of Mom's favorites. None of the regular white & yellow daisies. The brightest, daisiest-like arrangement out on display was dominated by all-yellow daisies, and they were as bright and cheery as it gets.

I bounced over to the card aisle and found the cheeriest selection there: a mug with a heart on it and a bouquet bursting out. *A little hug for you today.*

In the heat of the car, I wrote on the blank inside:

I wish you peace, Mama.

Love,

Chickie-Dee

I pushed open the side door, which always stuck a little, and Mom's blocky desk hit me like the blast of A/C. The desk where I wrote the letter, in the same room Gret's broad thick tail always swept low and wide after she'd jumped down from her front window seat perch where she'd watch my car pull in. How had she always known I was coming home?

Last night I had the greatest dream about Gretchen (well, any dream/visit from Gretor is great.) Basically I walked in the back door of Mom's and Gret came to see me, all crouching and slit-eyed and wagging her tail. I loved and petted her like I used to and told her I was so glad she was back and that I had a little more time with her.

Oh my God I love her so much.

Diary entry, August 9, 2004

Top to bottom: Gretchen waiting at the window for me; Snuggling by the door, c· 1994; Ready for a walk, January 1997

I crept through, down the hall and into the open space of the kitchen, where I had always hooked up Gret for our walks. In winter, I'd put on her baseball cap to match my fuzzy winter one that tied around my ears for campus walks.

"Going for a W-A-L-K?" Mom would ask to prevent her from going nutty if the answer was no. But before long, Gretchen had learned the spelling, and it became, "Are you gonna take her for a you-know-what?"

"Hi Mom!" I yelled, dropping my keys on the island butcher block.

"Chick!?" she replied from her bedroom.

I kept going, through the family room and down the hall, giving a peek into my old bedroom. The shiny blue bean bag was still by my bed. I pictured her sitting in it as I read or did homework or watched TV, her paws dangling. Putting my finger in her mouth when she yawned (The one thing I did to annoy her!). The spot on her tongue. The blanket I put on her, cinched around her face like a babushka. Yawning some more, and sinking down in a fetal position; gritting the beans as she repositioned herself in the middle of the night.

On my nightstand stood the pink floral fabric framed pictures of Gret in my best friend Jessica's bedroom, a sheepish look in her eyes because we'd coaxed her up onto the bed. She came so far, from the kitchen newspaper Bill made her sleep on as a pup, worried she'd pee on the carpets. When she had proven herself house-trained, she graduated to a dog bed next to the sliding door. I had tiptoed down those first nights and laid my head on hers. I had finally had my real live someone to care for and teach ("sit" and "shake" with her dainty little paw.), so much better than the cabbage patch dolls. We'd listen to the wailing moan of the train horn and beared childhood together. She'd breathe and stretch it off, deep and long.

In her new life in the sprawling, skylit ranch, Gretchen had sauntered freely and found a bed wherever we slept. She had still only needed to give a whimper to go out and her signature knock on the door with her nails when she was ready to come in.

Sleepy times at home in Southwick, c· 1994

I pulled myself away from my old bedroom door to find Mom at her bedroom door in her red plaid bathrobe. She looked as tired as she sounded, her face pale, the contours of bags under eyes noticeable. The usual joy had been sucked out by "too much craziness."

I handed her the flowers and card, which she began to open.

"That's it," she said. "I just want peace."

I bobbed my head, and hugged her tight.

"Thank you, Chick," she said, smelling the flowers. "They're beautiful. You're a perfect child."

"I'll put them in water," I said, taking them.

"Let me take my shower and we'll have a fresh cup."

I set up the flowers on the butcher block and wandered back to the family room. Feeling a little dazed from waking up late, I dropped onto the big blue leather couch and grabbed at the coffee table for one of the leftover *People* Magazines from Bill's office. Julia Roberts was having twins. Laci Peterson's murder trial. Mom watched it nonstop on Court TV.

I yawned, rolled over onto the cold blue leather toward the back of the couch to block the sunlight pouring in from the skylight and the wall-length glass windows that blended into the slider. I tried to settle my mind and remember last night's dreams, and noticed the song was still playing. "When You Believe." It had been playing in the back of my brain all morning. I turned onto my back and dropped a decorative horse pillow over my eyes. Laying on my back is always when I do my best thinking— or should I say, *not* thinking. It always seemed to move my focus to my gut more and bring important things to the forefront.

I should go to her.

While Mom is in the shower, while no one is here. I can get teary and sad and Mom won't see me like that.

I'm not napping anyway.

I pulled myself up and glided to the butcher block, pulled up on one from the inside of the bunch—a bright yellow flower that matched the "Rooster Rescue" T-shirt I was wearing, a gift from Mom on her Key West trip. A piece of me and Mom for Gretchen.

I walked slowly, on the same path we took over five years ago. Bill had chosen a spot behind the woodpile, the most prominent landmark of the yard, just off the path that went to the brook. I had agreed through sobs, and followed Cookie and Bill as they carried her and took turns digging. I only carried the pain and the goodbye letter:

Friday, July 2, 1999

Dear Gretchen,

I love you more than anything in this world. You have been the best dog to me, a best friend and sister and daughter. You got me through losing Oliver and my first home! You got me through life on our new hill!

Dear Gretchen

You asked nothing of me, and nothing felt better than showering my love on you. You made me so happy just lying next to me while I studied. And lying next to you is the greatest peace on earth. So much love and we never had to say a word!

I had so much fun running with you and watching you wade into the pond and make the frogs jump, and not letting you in til you dried off on the deck. Sock game with you was the funnest. I won't tell Mom you scratched the foot of the dining room table. It was my fault for not clipping your nails, anyway.

I loved our drives with the windows down and Tom Petty playing, even though you hated the car and shook the whole time. When you stuck your head between the seats and rode along beside me with the breeze coming in, that was heaven.

Now nothing will be the same. How can I even go on? I can't have kids without you. How COULD I without you beside me?

I'll love you forever and ever, and I will NEVER forget you.
LOVE,
Your girl,
Heidi

I opened the sliding door—always a tug—and made my way toward the woodpile. I navigated through scrub, stepping high to stomp it down and over the low edge of the woodpile, holding a thin tree for balance. I crunched through the brown of the forest floor and took the chance to scan for color. Purple? Red? Yellow? *You could make a wildflower grow here, too, Gret.* The song played. The ending now; the chorus. Whitney and Mariah together. I pictured the video: They're crouched toward each other, bouncing, finger-pointing, belting it out. And I spotted the stone rectangle that was Gretchen's gravestone.

Gretchen's gravestone, Southwick

Bill had a client with a monument business who had done the stone, and we had chosen the words together with Mom. *A Great Dog*, because we hadn't wanted anyone to think there was a human buried there. *Alive in Memory*, because I had very strongly wanted to say that *something* was alive about my dog, and memory was the only thing I could come up with.

I knelt before the stone, wiped away a stray pine needle, and placed the long-stem of the yellow flower under the words, *Alive in Memory*, on top of a shriveled purple flower I left last time. I hung my head down, nearly touching my forehead to the flower, and tried not to cry this time. I looked up, around the forest, trying to hold back the sadness and focus on the good times.

Gretor I love you, I began. *And still you're very much alive in memory.*

But the tears still came.

I closed my eyes, and breathed in, and out, and listened to Mariah and Whitney.

I do believe.

I rose up, still listening, over the woodpile to the sunlit grass, and wiped my eyes. I decided on the long way, along the grass line by Bill's little garden and the raspberry bushes. Any wildflowers there? I stared off before taking a few steps back toward the house. And that's when I heard Mom shrieking.

"CHICKIE!!!!!"

I looked up, and saw her panicky face poked out from the slider, bathrobe still on, her hair damped down.

"YEAH?" I said across the lawn.

"HEIDI!!!!' She shrieked again, and began to yell under her breath. "What are you doing? Come here. GET IN HERE!!!"

My feet began to respond as my mind searched. *What happened?*

"Chickie!" She said, meeting me half-way across the grass in her Dearfoam slippers, breathing hard, holding my shoulders.

"I just saw Gretchen walking next to you!"

Mom was frantic, almost pleading, scared.

"What?"

"Chickie," Mom said, calmer, "She was right next to you, prancing and looking up at you, just like she used to."

"I was just at her grave," I explained, tears rushing out. "I brought her a flower. I was asking her for a sign. I have been, for days now."

"Oh my God. I walked out from the bathroom thinking you were in the house, and I was half paying attention, and saw you and Gret through the window. Let's go inside."

We stood at the butcher block beside Mom's flowers, and let the idea wash over us, let the feelings come: joy, gratitude, *relief.*

She's with me. She's OK. We're OK. I'd been flailing at sea, searching for my beloved and half drowning myself, and finally a vessel captained by Mom and Gretchen herself pulled me on.

I looked to the tile floor.

Gret could be right here with me, right now, just like she just was.

"She was right next to me?" I asked, speaking words I never thought I'd say. "What side was she on?"

"She was right alongside you as she always did, trotting and looking up at you. Doot, doot, doot."

She held her hands up and pointed her index fingers down, making the prancing motion as she said it.

"And her nose was up sniffing at the air. Three steps. Doot, doot, doot, and then she was gone."

"Did she look good?" I asked.

"She looked like she did in her prime—not old. It wasn't exactly like she was right there, it was a little opaque/muted, like she was 90% there."

Mom came to me and wrapped me in her bathrobed arms, peace poured over me—Gretchen's pure peace that I didn't realize how much I missed—and we did our little dance, our heads bobbing higher than usual.

"Chickie," she said, stepping back, glassy-eyed. "I totally, 100% believe now, in all this spirit stuff."

"Me too."

I am the luckiest!!! To have such
an amazing, good spirit w/ me.
Diary entry, January 21, 2005

I can't believe how much has changed in 5 years. Last time I wrote, Gretor had just died and things were so raw. I was heartbroken—for almost five years. Missed her terribly and wondered how she was, where she was. Felt guilty that I should have lived with her, stayed at Mom's til the end. Felt guilty for being insensitive toward the end (not at the end) cause I knew the day was coming and I maybe emotionally (and physically) detached to try to spare myself grief. But nothing I could do could spare me from the incredible grief of losing someone so close. Anyway, it's all a moot point now because I know Gretor is safe & good and I'm at peace.

It was a miracle, a prayer answered.

Diary entry, January 21, 2005

9

Going On

December 21, 2005

Baby Kevin,

I'm at your Grammy's house — your dad, Grammy & Bill,
Nellie and kids went to Bright Nights (Christmas light display)
at Forest Park. There wasn't room in the van for all of us so I
decided to spend some quiet time here (You just kicked!). My
dog Gretchen and I spent some good times here—chasing around
the dining room table with a sock, (You moved again!), greeting
at the door all excited, going for walks around the neighborhood

(You couldn't say the word "walk" if you didn't mean it!).
Gretor was/is the best and I bet she's THRILLED that I am
having a baby. I never thought I could go on with my life (and
have kids) without her but now I know she's around and taking
part in things. She will watch over you, for sure (in a dream I
saw her watching over your cousin Logan).

Now your beautiful [ultrasound] pictures are on the fridge
here. Grammy called me at work Monday just to say that she
wants to kiss the back of your neck (that's her favorite picture)
and why can't you get here sooner?!

It really won't be long now and I can't believe it. I feel so
lucky to be having a baby of my own—could it really be? I have
to pinch myself. Yesterday the doctor examined me and said
that your head was really far down—you are getting ready!
There are so many people waiting for you. You will be loved,
stimulated, and nurtured. We love you so much already.

Your dad brought your cradle up last weekend when I was in
Boston with Grammy, Cookie, and Nell. (He also painted three
rooms so our house is cozier). I just have to put the mattress
and sheet in and get you a snuggly warm thing for your
carseat—which your dad is getting installed tomorrow while I'm

at work. Work had a shower for me (you) last Wednesday and now your bed is covered with more stuff! Have to work on that over this Christmas.

It will be our last lonely Christmas. There's a little stroller ornament with nothing but a lonely tree sitting in it, hanging on our new lil' tree on the piano. Can't wait to meet you—I pray now that you arrive safely.

Love,

Mom

January 30, 2006

Dear Baby Kevin,

You're here!!! I still can't quite believe it. You came 12 days early so it was a surprise. I left things hanging at work.

...

[When] they brought you to me, all naked and still wet, your hair looked curly. You were kind of pale. I stared at you in amazement and cried to hold you for the first time. (Now you are grunting in your lil' chair and your hat is falling off.) It was all a lot to take in but I was so happy that you arrived safely. You're perfect and as expected, the cutest and sweetest thing I've ever seen (OK—maybe tied w/ Gretchen)—that's saying a lot!

You were born 7 lbs. 2 oz.

At 7:20 p.m.

You're a Capricorn—I hear a good sign—a leader.

Love,

Mom

It took me years to realize a connection between the date of Gretchen's passing (7/2/99) and the numbers surrounding Kevin's birth. I believe it was Gretchen's way of marking his birth with her presence and blessing.

EPILOGUE

Back to the Hill
May 2015

Kevin did not want to go. He wanted to play basketball. So I set off on my own, letting my bike coast past the grand finale of the spring flowers, past the greenest trees and lawns, birdsong all around.

I braked when the blue house appeared around the corner. The trees Bill had planted out front now towered over the driveway where I shot solitary hoops and sat idly in my first car. The porch slung back into darkness to the front door where we had filed in that first day in 1984. I found the pedal with my foot and veered down the next side street. No need to weird out the neighbors with staring.

I took a left and a quick right at the TAG SALE sign, onto the street that made a semicircle around our neighborhood and perched atop the bluff overlooking the shops down on the main drag. I'd seen the sign driving earlier and, knowing who lived here, did a drive by. I knew the house.

I pumped my legs and felt the burn. They hadn't had this workout in thirty years. I parked my bike the end of the driveway of the colonial and noticed the backyard, just as stately as the house. What a view it must be, past the trees.

I turned to the tables lined up and browsed blankly as another customer cleared out.

"Claudia?" I said as she futzed with the newspapers and plastic bags under her table.

"Yes?"

"I'm Heidi, Jessica's friend. Remember?"

"Oh of course!"

"How are you?" I asked. "You look the same!"

"Well that's a good thing! We're good," she said. "We're actually moving. New Hampshire."

"Oh! And I just moved back!" I said, pointing to the rest of the neighborhood which had been expanded and connected to the next. It was the reason we moved to

Southwick. Mom had had enough and yearned for privacy. "I can't believe how things have changed!"

"I know," she said. "How are your parents?"

"Good. Mom and Bill are still in Southwick, but they're thinking of moving again, too." I said, spotting a Brown University mug. "Somewhere smaller and more manageable. Well I'll just browse around."

"Please do," Claudia said. "We're not taking any of this with us."

I shopped the things of a family's life: stuffed animals, kid's books, slippers that didn't fit, still in the box. Keepsakes they no longer had a shelf for.

"Did you get this when you were there for the swim meet?" I asked, holding the mug. "when you found Gretchen?"

"Oh no, my husband is an alumnus."

I laid out the Beatrix Potter story collection, a tan Pound Puppies stuffed animal dog just like one I used to have, and three dollars.

"Thank you," I said. "You changed my life."

"Oh," she said. "I wasn't just going to leave a *puppy* in a *parking lot.*"

I'd heard her say that before.

"I know, but really," I said, my eyes filling, "I needed Gretchen so bad. It's like you brought her straight *to* me! She's the reason I do the work I do now. I need to give you a hug!"

Claudia met me halfway in a smiley, tight one. I put the things in my backpack and wished her a happy retirement before speeding back, past the old blue house again. I slowed down and peered back to where Gretchen's run was and the picnic table next to it where I'd sit with her. Now a shed. *But she could be* with *me, right now,* I thought, gaining speed. *Probably is. On a bike like this had been the only time I could begin to keep up with her.* She was probably there running like a puppy, sniffing up at me and the wind, hovering on God's earth she had lived to run and breathe in. It may have been a maze of new pavement and strange people to me back in the day, but with Hugo, Gretchen had her own world of forest and rivers. A bird shot across road in front of me. I was in the world Gretchen lived in again. A bigger, better world.

I passed the limits of our old romps, past new white sidewalks and perfectly manicured mcmansions, to my new life in a different older neighborhood. I looked ahead to see the silhouettes of willowy Kevin shooting hoops and his sister CeeCee, a lab/husky mix lurching herself from the tie-out at the front door. She barked her head off, demanding I come see her first, dropping her body to the ground as I approached to reveal the flash of white on her belly that said, *pet here.* I dropped my knees down with her, rubbing scratchy white with one hand, cradling her soft forehead in the other, kissing the smoothed black fur of her temple, and breathing in the good old smell of *dog.*

When I arose, baby AJ dangled in his daddy's arms behind me in his *Little Brother* onesie with big and little foxes on it.

"I got you something, AJ!" I said, dropping the backpack to the grass and squeezing my treasure out from between the zipper.

He reached out to the soft, black-nosed face of the Pound Puppy, and his sparkly blue eyes smiled.

One More Letter

July 2, 2015

Dear Gretchen,

It's been 16 years since I had to say goodbye! I was a wreck. I really thought that was it and we'd be apart. I wrote to you that day that I didn't want to go on, I didn't want to have kids if you weren't around.

And today, I have two beautiful boys and know you're still with us. You've shown that, and your mark was stamped on Kevin's day of birth. Thank you for showing me it was OK to go on. I'm sure you wanted me to. I'm sure you've been guiding me. I love you as much as ever honey. My sister and kindred spirit. I've been through a lot and have gone cold a lot, but you still bring me to tears. How you led me and saved me. There aren't many you meet in life that do those things for you and who you connect with so deeply.

I played "sock game" with Kevin this morning and smiled for you. I drank from the I Love My Dog mug. It's as true as ever! You'll always be my dog and I hope to always be your human.

🤍🐾 my Gretchen.

Love,

Heidi

Note on my iPhone

At the grave placing flowers with my sons,
before Mom and Bill's move from Southwick, February 2017

Lounging at our second home at Jessica's, c· 1986

Dear Gretchen

Author's Note

"I have a story for you..."

In the years following August 2004, I shared Gretchen's miracle sparingly: with close friends and colleagues, when pets had passed, or whenever discussions turned to death and dying. I wanted it to give hope to others.

People responded with goosebumps. It seemed to take them away from the depressing place in which I used to dwell, in thoughts of my loved ones' frozen graves that seemed so far from Heaven. It seemed to take their mind to a new and exciting realm of happy possibilities, which is what I want for you, my reader.

The most important thing I learned from these events is this:

If I could be that miserable walking through life while the most beautiful thing was happening alongside me, then I was sorely out of touch with a whole other side of reality that was the key to my healing. I get the sense that most of us live life in this state, cut off from the spiritual world. I hope this story is a step toward opening your eyes to it and toward ramping up your own belief that your loved ones still walk with you after physical death. I found that belief is an important first step toward a miracle, and miracles can happen to any one of us, any day.

There have been other miracles since that warm August 2004 day. After my first marriage ended, I met a man named Al on a return flight home from Washington, D.C. We got talking about our work, and he explained that his dog, Goliath, had passed six months earlier. We became two strangers crying together, and I found myself sharing Gretchen's story. We married in 2013, and got a dog named CeeCee. One night, Al thought he saw CeeCee sitting and watching over me as I slept. He went to pat her, and his hand fell to the bed. It was my Gretchen, still with me years later.

I now look at Gretchen's physical death as a voyage to a Heaven much closer than what I was taught as a kid, as a place with geographic restriction, high above the clouds.

The bond does not break when a loved one is away.

I believe that the happiness and peace I regained through the events of this story is what Gretchen always wanted for me. Our pets love us so deeply, yet we often question it after they're gone. Of course they still love us. Why *wouldn't* they continue to want our happiness and peace after they've gone on their voyage?

Two months after my mother helped me with this story, she went on her own voyage. What she showed me about life after death helped me cope, but I still had to reorient myself on the earth. As with Gretchen's passing, I asked a lot of *Hows. How can this be? How am I supposed to go on without her?* I miss her voice and her touch. I go into slumps of sadness and have to remind myself of my own advice, which at times I don't want to hear, because we sometimes just need to be sad and cry.

My advice is this: Keep talking to your loved ones. Make time for quiet so you can listen. Look for signs from them in everyday life: birds, songs, even bumper stickers. One sign from my mom—which came multiple times, to more than one of her children—brought a wave of relief and comfort that lingered for weeks. The sign was a pineapple, and from my mom, the boat captain, it didn't take much to connect it to the legend that New England sea captains placed pineapples on their doorsteps as a sign that they'd reached home after a long voyage.

With belief, observation, and prayer, we bridged the gap between physical and spiritual. We honored the bonds of love. It's a practice available to us all.

Dear Gretchen

About the Author

Photo: Sarah Giusti

Heidi Parker Colonna is a lifelong animal welfare advocate, writer, and teacher. She writes for the children's magazine, *Kind News*, published by RedRover. She's written for publications such as *All Animals* and *Animal Sheltering* and was contributing editor for *Humane Activist* Magazine. Her writing on the themes of family and faith has appeared in *Pregnancy & Newborn Magazine*'s blog and the Red Lion Inn's *Lion's Tales: A Collection of Shorts*. She lives in Massachusetts with her husband, Al, sons Kevin and AJ, and husky/black lab mix CeeCee. She is working on other books for all ages. Learn more and connect at www.parkercolonna.com.

Dear Gretchen

www.ingramcontent.com/pod-product-compliance
Lightning Source LLC
Chambersburg PA
CBHW020417130626
46549CB00006B/2611